T 8125

20317

Courteous Kids

Thank You

By Janine Amos   Illustrated by Annabel Spenceley

Gareth Stevens Publishing
A WORLD ALMANAC EDUCATION GROUP COMPANY

Please visit our web site at: www.garethstevens.com
For a free color catalog describing Gareth Stevens'
list of high-quality books and multimedia programs,
call 1-800-542-2595 (USA) or 1-800-461-9120 (Canada).
Gareth Stevens Publishing's Fax: (414) 332-3567.

Library of Congress Cataloging-in-Publication Data

Amos, Janine.
      Thank you / by Janine Amos; illustrated by Annabel Spenceley.
        p. cm. — (Courteous kids)
      Includes bibliographical references.
      ISBN 0-8368-2807-0 (lib. bdg.)
      1. Gratitude—Juvenile literature. 2. Children—Conduct of life.
[1. Gratitude. 2. Etiquette. 3. Conduct of life.] I. Spenceley,
Annabel, ill. II. Title.
BJ1533.G8A46   2001
395.1'22—dc21   00-049298

This edition first published in 2001 by
Gareth Stevens Publishing
A World Almanac Education Group Company
330 West Olive Street, Suite 100
Milwaukee, WI 53212 USA

Gareth Stevens editor: Anne Miller
Cover design: Joel Bucaro

This edition © 2001 by Gareth Stevens, Inc. First published by Cherrytree Press,
a subsidiary of Evans Brothers Limited. © 1999 by Cherrytree (a member of the
Evans Group of Publishers), 2A Portman Mansions, Chiltern Street, London
W1M 1LE, United Kingdom. This U.S. edition published under license from
Evans Brothers Limited. Additional end matter © 2001 by Gareth Stevens, Inc.

Printed in the United States of America

1 2 3 4 5 6 7 8 9 05 04 03 02 01   2 0 3 1 7

Paul's Birthday

Today is Paul's birthday.

He is having a party.

Paul's grandma gives him a present.
Paul forgets to say "thank you."

6

He goes to play with his friends.
How does Grandma feel?

When Paul opens his present,
he remembers to say "thank you."

Paul gives Grandma a big hug.

How does Grandma feel now?

Joel's Spaceship

Joel is trying to build a spaceship.
It's hard work, and he is having trouble.

His brother, Scott, offers to help.
They build it together.

13

The spaceship is finished.

Joel forgets to tell Scott "thank you."

How does Scott feel?

Look!

Joel shows the spaceship to his dad.

Joel remembers that Scott helped him.

Joel thanks Scott.

How does Scott feel now?

Leah's Mom

Leah's friends come to play at her house.
Leah's mom gives them some juice.

She also makes them a snack.

Leah's mom helps them play dress up.

It's time for Leah's friends to go home.
They forget to say "thank you."

25

How does Leah's mom feel?
Leah thinks about it.

Leah thanks her mom.

The other children thank her, too.

How does Leah's mom feel now?

30

31

More Books to Read

Barney Says, "Please and Thank You." Stephen White
  (Lyrick Studios)

Manners. Aliki (Greenwillow)

Monster Manners: A Guide to Monster Etiquette.
  Bethany Roberts (Clarion)

The Thingumajig Book of Manners. Irene Keller
  (Ideals Childrens Books)

Note to Parents and Teachers

The questions that appear in **boldface** type can be used to initiate
discussion with your children or class. Encourage them to think of
possible answers before continuing with the story.

Additional Resources

Parents and teachers may find these materials useful in discussing
manners with children:

Video: *Manners Can Be Fun!* (ETI-KIDS, Ltd.)
  This video includes a teacher's guide.

Web Site: *Preschoolers Today: Where Have the Manners Gone?*
  www.preschoolerstoday.com/resources/articles/manners.htm